AF269122

OWN YOUR CRISIS

7 Steps To Mastering Your Inner Voice and Taking Ownership of Your Life

Karl Davis

Own Your Crisis
Copyright © 2020 by Karl Davis

ISBN: 978-1-8381016-0-2 (Paperback)

OWN YOUR CRISIS

7 Steps To Mastering Your Inner Voice and Taking Ownership of Your Life

Karl Davis

Acknowledgement

I want to thank God for taking the pen when I needed Him. I want to thank my Mother and Father for their continued support, and guidance. Thank you to my Brother and Sister for their encouragement. And thank you to my future Wife for her endless support, belief, and love.

Contents

Introduction

10, 9, 8, 7, 6, 5, 4, 3, 2 ,1… Pop goes the champagne, a happy new year, and a new you. This book was written during the quarantine period from a wooden cabin in the year of the 2020 global pandemic. My name is Karl, and I experienced it living in London, England. It's a year that sent a wave of crisis across the world. The wrath of the pandemic swept across the world, having a global effect. It affected the lives of many as unemployment rates were flying through the roof and thousands of people were suffering the loss of loved ones. All non-essential businesses were being forced to close their doors by the government. This pushed millions of people worldwide into a financial crisis they may never have seen coming when the champagne popped at the beginning of the year. The excitement at the beginning of 2020 was very high. People were talking about their new '20:20 vision' for their year ahead; however, this was swiftly becoming more and more blurry. There was a wonderful hope in the atmosphere at the beginning of the year, but it was slowly diminishing as months went by. It seemed as though everyday routines, holidays, business projections, and the whole world was coming to an abrupt halt. It felt as if a reset button had been clicked. No one knew how things would be from that point onwards or how they would adapt to their new normal. Even though we all know there's no promise to live without trials and tribulations, it can still be difficult to deal with the problems when they do come.

With this book, I hope to provide you with another reference point when you may experience a crisis in your life. Maybe you're at the quarter-life crisis stage when you are trying to figure out what you are going to do in life. Maybe your friend has bought this book for you as you've just come out of a relationship you thought would last forever. You could be in a severely tough financial situation, and you can't see the light at the end of the tunnel yet. Maybe you're unhappy with your life at the moment and are hungry for things to improve. Or maybe you have sadly lost someone close to you, and now you don't know how you will get through life without them. Some of these examples are challenges I have faced myself and know all too well. In fact, there are many forms of heart-wrenching periods in our lives that we could call a crisis or life-changing moment. I'll teach you how to take ownership of your crisis and how to come out the other side stronger. I'll go through the seven steps to take when faced with a crisis.

We all know when the effect of a crisis is weighing us down. This is something we struggle to forget for the rest of our lives. Your situation, past or present, is completely unique to you. You might remember the month or day it happened, who you were with, or other details that paint the picture in your mind immediately. During a crisis, we may feel a sense of overwhelming pressure come upon us due to the shock and the changes it brings to our lives. When we are under pressure, we experience the feeling of being pushed out of our comfort zone. Then our mental toughness is tested, and you get to see how well you can handle it. Most people don't like leaving their comfort zone in general, but, the truth is it's outside the comfort zone that the real magic in life happens. It's in the periods of uncertainty and change that we begin to gain a better understanding of ourselves.

With that being said, I'll take you into step one, which is Be Resourceful. Be sure to make use of the note's pages at the back of the book. It will be great for you to reflect back on your notes at a later date, so you can see how much you've developed since today.

Step One: Be Resourceful

Step one is about resourcefulness during the time of struggle. This is thinking about how creative you can get in a crisis and being resourceful with everything you have. This means you focus less on your needs and more on what you have at the present moment. How do you react in a crisis situation? You might think, "How am I supposed to act anyway?" One thing that often fascinates me is animals and their instinct for survival. One animal that amazes me most is the eagle. Why an eagle? Well, the truth is bird spotting is not my sport. However, I cannot forget when I heard an elder speak on staying strong when you have the most resistance against you. He went on to say, "Most regular birds can fly at 10,000 feet, but an eagle has the ability to fly at 39,000 feet." When there's a storm, regular birds are likely to hibernate as the winds become too strong for them to fly as they normally do, but the eagle choses to use the storm to its advantage by locking each wing in position to soar in the wind. What's great about this is in the eye of a storm, the eagle thrives and uses the storm to fiercely rise to new heights. The representation of soaring when the storm comes can sound a lot easier said than done. This is where it must come from within to make a shift in your mindset. The best advice to take from the example of the eagle is to mirror its courage in the storm. The eagle uses the same resistance (wind) that could hold it back and turns it into a weapon to lift it to much higher heights. I think we could definitely take a leaf or two out of the eagle's book and, when possible, use our adversities to our advantage.

There is so much power in becoming

resourceful in times of struggle. Sometimes we are too busy looking at what we want or need that we forget about what we already have in the grasp of our hand. How can you be more like the eagle and use what is against you as a spring board to take you to new heights? As I said in the introduction, this book was written during the quarantine period in London, where people were instructed by the government to stay home. This meant people were spending the most time they've ever spent in their lives at home. The quarantine period was a crisis in itself, much less the viral enemy that was causing countless deaths and sickness around the world. The quarantine caused normalcy to be massively shifted since schools, nightclubs, pubs, churches, live sporting events, and the list goes on were all closed until further notice. If you are reading this years down the line and thinking this is all too hard to imagine, I can tell you it was definitely true. In this time period, people suddenly had a lot more time on their hands. This resulted in people becoming more resourceful, just like the eagle soaring through the storm. By living in a time where they had less things to do and less places to go, many people reconnected with the closest people around them. Some people who did little exercise since the early 2000s started doing daily workouts on group video calls. Some parents got to see their children again, who may live in the same house as them but never actually see them much. A lot of families and friends drew closer virtually in a time when everything got stripped back. Life suddenly had less distractions. This was a good lesson that you can in fact do more with less. It really starts with how you look at things, whether you only view it as your freedom being taken away or a chance to be creative with all the resources you have.

In the midst of adversity, a key thing that you need to be aware of is your mindset of resourcefulness. This means thinking clearly about your options under pressure as a clouded head is difficult to use when you are making important decisions. In a crisis, it's important to be aware of how and what you are thinking. It's important to find a positive suggestion in a not-so-positive situation. Awareness is always an important first step before trying to improve anything. Our minds and day-to-day thoughts are often dominated by whatever we give the majority of our attention. If you live in fear of something, there is most definitely a root to it, which is feeding that fear of yours. There was a study on six to fourteen month old babies carried out in 1960 that found we are only born with two innate fears—one being the fear of loud noises and the other being the fear of falling. Often people have a fear of change. This fear comes about when you realise things may never be the same, and you're fearful of what the future holds. This could be staying in your current job that you're tired of because you can't stand your boss. Sometimes it feels like the easier option is to stay. Staying put means you don't have to look for another opportunity and adapt to a new environment. It just seems like the safest thing to do. However, remaining in a safe and comfortable position has also lead to millions of people having regrets later in life. Therefore, it's important to recognise when you're in fear of changing your current normal. Instead, you must face the obstacles and be resourceful at the same time. Essentially, you must always try to adapt to the new challenges that life brings.

To take you to new heights like the eagle, you might find you already have everything you need around you to get started. Since the first step is be resourceful, it's important to show gratitude for the things you do have. Gratitude is a must. It's when we appreciate the smaller things that we open up our eyes to new perspectives. An increased level of joy will arise when you wake up in the morning, and be thankful that you're still breathing. Regardless of how good or bad you feel your life is, someone elsewhere is fighting to stay alive. If you're breathing that means you still have a purpose to live out. Another reason to be grateful is for the people around you, your nearest and dearest. You may not always see eye to eye all the time, but that doesn't mean you shouldn't make the effort to spend some quality time with them.

Time was such an interesting thing during the quarantine period. At times, it felt as if there were suddenly more hours in a day and more days in a week. It was almost as if we had way too much time, and for the first few weeks, there was a struggle to adapt to this abundance of time. With all this newly found time, it called upon resourcefulness and creativity. During the time period where people were told to stay home, they truly learnt how to be more resourceful. People were no longer allowed to go out for non-essential tasks. They could only exercise and go food shopping. This rule didn't apply for key workers, who were the nurses, carers, shop assistants, and emergency services as they went to work as normal. People with young children, who may have been too young to comprehend the situation, suddenly had to make home the fun place to be, the place to study (schools being closed), and much more. This is when resourcefulness came alive across the nation. In the midst of a crisis, parents found all types of creative ways to keep their children entertained at home. On social media, there were mini dry ski slopes created in peoples gardens, family dance routines going viral, and so much more. This new way of life encouraged a renewed sense of community as people tried to keep their peace as much as possible whilst adapting to their new reality.

Sometimes it takes a crisis to notice the things we take for granted. The good thing is it's in our human nature to be more creative when we have limited resources. It's when we are forced to be resourceful that our survival instinct kicks in, and with less, you begin to do more.

Step Two: Be Kind To Yourself

#BeKind became a trending hashtag after a British television Presenter sadly took her own life. This encouraged people to speak up about the importance of being kind. This trending hashtag related more to being kind to each other on the internet. However, this also applies to how you speak to yourself. In the midst of your crisis, it's not good to beat yourself up over your present reality because that will not change anything for you. Isn't it a great quality when someone remains kind to you even when they have a good reason to be angry? It takes strength to be kind when your nerves are being tested. Sometimes we need to do the right thing, even when every bone in our body is telling us to do the opposite. It's these moments when you begin to feel a new sense of growth and maturity.

To be kind to yourself, you need to be less harsh with your words. One of the most damaging things in the world is comparison. It is a thief of your joy. Comparison makes people question things like, "Why don't I have that?" or "Why is my body not like that?" This only leads down the path of unhappiness, less motivation in life, and feeling negative about yourself.

How can you be more kind to yourself? A good first step to take is to exercise some compassion towards yourself. Often, people compare themselves to someone else based on the job they do, how much more money they have, or the lifestyle they are living, and the truth is, everyone's journey in life is unique to them. Therefore, you need to focus more on your journey and where you're going rather than spending too much time looking left and right and not moving forward.

Becoming more compassionate towards yourself is a huge step in eliminating comparison. Compassion opens up opportunities as it allows you to find a sense of acceptance of yourself. In turn, this brings you into a more peaceful mindset on a daily basis. With more peace, your mind can function at its best. You can make rational decisions rather than acting on emotion. You're at your optimum mind-state when you don't put unnecessary pressures on yourself to be perfect. Pressure to be perfect isn't good, as it makes you constantly scared to make a mistake. Mistakes will happen, and if they do, that's usually a good sign that you had the guts to go for something. When you view a mistake as a learning experience, this is a great way to show compassion towards yourself. And just to be clear, compassion is far from throwing a pity party for yourself or avoiding difficult topics. Compassion is about you holding yourself accountable for your mistakes but also forgiving yourself, being kind, and not holding on to negative feelings.

Forgiving yourself is a release from being caught up in a situation that you can no longer change. You need to make a conscious decision with yourself to forgive the wrongs you have done. Unforgiveness is like a nasty poison that begins to eat away at you on the inside. The best way to release yourself from that bondage is to choose to forgive. By doing this, you will find you're able to live a much happier and pure-hearted life.

Maybe it's a good time for you to pause and think about how well you have forgiven yourself. How do you react when you mess up, don't get something done that you planned, or aren't where you want to be in life? How kind are you to yourself in these scenarios? Who is where they want to be anyway? Stop beating yourself up about that. You'll find when you do have all the zeros in your bank account, when you buy that new car, or when you lose those extra pounds from Christmas, you'll most likely need something else to make you happy. I totally agree that it's a great thing to be ambitious and to want more in life as those are honourable characteristics. Even the fact that you're reading this book shows you are conscious of your growth. However, it does become a problem when your joy is taken from your life if you haven't reached your goals. This can quite easily lead down a very negative path. So, it's better to take more productive steps on improving certain areas of your life without that being your only source of happiness. Set out your productive steps today instead of being locked in a stage of paralysis analysis, which means analysing your life over and over but not making steps that move the needle forward.

In a study done by psychologist, Susan David, she supported 'Be Kind To Yourself' by stating, "How we deal with our inner life is everything." She went on to say, "Research shows the radical acceptance of all our emotions, even the difficult ones, is the cornerstone to resilience, thriving, and true authentic happiness." This statement shows it's important for you to accept your emotions rather than feel sorry for yourself or ignore them. When we do this, we build up our emotional fitness, and in return, we become stronger on the inside. Susan David went on to say that one of the best pieces of advice she received was being told to "Write down what you're thinking on a piece of paper, and write as if no one was ever going to read it." This might be a refreshing, or even a scary experience to see all your thoughts in front of you in general, and even more so in the midst of a crisis. By writing down what you're thinking, you can acknowledge the emotions and access what your inner self is craving. When you are kind to yourself, you come to an acceptance of your imperfections. It also allows you to live a life of less clutter where you're not weighed down by your thoughts. In turn, this will have a positive impact on the quality of your relationships with the closest people around you.

Being kind to yourself is all about being

conscious of how you care about yourself and finding what works for you as an individual. Some people work out their problems in the gym by exerting energy and relieving stress at the same time. Some people kneel down at their bed in prayer to find peace within and speak positive words over their life. Other people may choose to ignore an issue, but that only makes you numb to the pain for that moment. Unfortunately, when you ignore it, the problem doesn't disappear. It builds up over time if it isn't dealt with sooner rather than later and this can turn into a big mountain of problems.

Essentially, it is important to focus on compassion and being kind to yourself. Having a sense of understanding towards yourself is crucial to your growth. It's important to be kind to you. This has a positive effect on how you treat others around you, so if you're not choosing to do it for yourself, at least do it with your loved ones in mind. Adopting more self-compassion will put you on the right path to taking ownership of your situation.

Step Three: Be in Control of Your Inner Thermometer

The third step is about gaining control of our emotions when times get tough. We can compare our inner thermometer to our emotions. The number of things we allow to affect us is set by how much we're in control of our emotions. We all know the feeling when we are speaking to someone, and they seem very much on edge. It always feels as if they would erupt like a volcano if one more wrong thing is said to them. It is often difficult to have a good conversation with someone like this as it feels like they are a ticking time bomb.

As mentioned previously, a global

pandemic took place as this was being written. World leaders were making life threatening decisions on a day-to-day basis. Lives were lost at insane rates, and people were panicking. This sent the world into a state of shock as people's normal had been flipped upside down. People began panic buying food and all the necessities. As crazy as it might seem, even toilet paper disappeared off the shelves. It was during a worldwide crisis like this that I realised how important it is to be aware of your emotions. I asked myself, "Am I the influencer or influencee of my emotions?" This made me think. Am I the one in charge of my emotions, or are they in charge of me? During a worldwide crisis, national news broadcasters advised people to limit the amount of news they watched. How crazy is that? This was probably as effective as the 'Smoking Kills' note on cigarette packets. The news injected more fear into the nation, and there wasn't much positive news being spread. In the quarantine period, I realised how important it is to control how much negative information we listen to. The reality was news broadcasters were telling people to stop watching too much news. Then it really hit home that we all need to be more aware of the words that we feed our minds as this affects the way we think and feel on a daily basis.

To influence my own emotions during this time, I made sure I limited my consumption of the news. I listened to it for an hour or so every couple days. It was still important to keep up to date with what was going on in the world around me. The difference was I no longer allowed it to consume me for hours each day. It was like a distressing reality TV show, which was very real. I personally found that cutting out a lot of the noise was a better way to keep peace in this storm. I found speaking about hope for better days was much more uplifting for my grandfather, who was going through the situation alone and feeling imprisoned in his own home. This pandemic wasn't easy for lots of people.

Controlling your 'inner thermometer'

matters in a crisis when you're leading or managing a company and know the business is going through a difficult spell. It is your duty to guide your team without them sensing fear of failure. Fear and lack of confidence can be smelt from a mile away. If you don't seem sure about what you're saying, then how in the world can your team believe what you're telling them? When you have setbacks, you still need to have a level-headed approach to whatever it is you're doing. When you are bold regardless of the setbacks, this gives your team the confidence that things will get better, and this is what attracts more growth. When you build up your inner strength, the external pressures begin to bounce off you that would have weighed you down before. This allows you to be proactive rather than reactive to your surroundings.

One thing for sure is being in control of your inner thermometer takes conscious practice. In an excerpt from a book called *Anointing Fall on Me*, the author, TD Jakes, speaks about his inner Holy Spirit being his thermostat and a thermometer at the same time. The job of a thermostat is to regulate the temperature in a building. It does this by sensing the air temperature and adjusting to the desired temperature. He went on to say, "It's the Holy Spirit that guides me in times when the atmosphere around me is hostile." He puts his trust in it to guide his decisions. The building thermostat and the Holy Spirit are similar in that they are there to help you regain control regardless of your environment. When you are faced with a problem, being able to control your inner thermometer is a valuable skill to have. This is something that will serve you well throughout your life.

So, how can you 'Be in Control of your Inner Thermometer'? In the moment of crisis, it's important to realise that fear and panic are the wrong roads to go down. Now I know that this can be a lot easier said than done. However, when you are fearful, this often leads to anxiousness and more struggle. It's better to face your fears, and that way, you make the problem smaller than you. I personally don't have an official bucket list, but one day I'd like to sky dive from an aeroplane. This is way outside of my comfort zone as I'm probably already the loudest on the big rollercoaster rides. However, right now, I already know the most scary moments will be everything that happens before I actually jump out of the plane. Once I've jumped, though, and begin to glide through the air, I already know all my fears will be a distant memory, and I would have wasted a lot of my time fearing and getting anxious. Who knows, I might even want to do it again. The main thing I want to show you is the importance of not getting consumed by your emotions in a crisis. Sometimes you will have to cut out all the noise. By doing this, you will have more focus, and you'll gain control of your inner thermometer. You'll begin to acknowledgement the fear and negativity as a waste of time and energy, and suddenly, you will realise your life is a little bit simpler than before.

Step Four: Be Hopeful

To be hopeful is having an expectation of a better future. This requires that you accept the present moment may be difficult for you, but you're still building up your hope for a better and brighter future. You might say, "But you don't understand the pain of my situation." Hope is an attitude and not always a feeling to start with. It is something that we actively have to generate more and more of over time. It doesn't come from you having one hopeful thought, and then everything magically changes. Hope is something that you have to consciously nurture over time, and I guarantee you will begin to see changes in your life. Hope is something you have to build up alongside the fear and doubts. It doesn't make your negative emotions disappear at the click of a finger. You will have to discipline yourself and consciously try to avoid thinking hopeless thoughts.

There are great benefits to being more hopeful. Studies have found that people who are optimists have better health, achieve more, and are a lot happier than pessimists. They found that optimistic people are more practical and are better at doing things to make a crisis situation easier to cope with. Another benefit of being hopeful is it allows you to have a more lighthearted approach to life. You will also find hopeful people are great to speak to about your missions in life. Hope brings a lifestyle shift and will reflect in everything you do, everything you say, and everything you are. Another great thing about hope is it provides the light in the darkness, and you have the capability to be that light for yourself and the people around you.

In the midst of the current global pandemic, they brought together religious leaders on national news to pray for nations of people and their government leaders. In a crisis like this, they knew nations needed a seed of hope and prayer for strength during the testing times. It gave enough belief that although times are tough, "This too shall pass." This was the encouragement that many people across the world needed. I'm sure this small seed of hope saved many lives and stopped people from losing complete hope of their precious life.

Some will say being hopeful is a waste of time. Maybe they'd rather not tease themselves by getting their hopes up over things. They might call themselves a realistic person and don't see the point of hoping for something that they cannot see happening. I'll say I'm a realistic optimist. A realistic optimist can approach a situation that's a problem with a little more balance. An example of this would be Person A saying, "Starting today, I'm going to train for one month for the Athletics

100 metres event, and I hope to beat Usain Bolt's world record." This would be a very optimistic and hopeful statement to make as this is something which took a lifetime of effort for Bolt to achieve. However, if Person B was to say, "Starting today, I'm going to train for one month for the Athletics 100 metres event. I will time myself every 10 days, and I hope to improve my personal best each time." Even though this is still something that would prove to be difficult, Person B is a lot more likely to achieve their goal. So, to be a realistic optimist, you are someone who is balancing a combination of practicality and hope.

Lots of people often turn to hope as their last resort. They begin to pray for things to improve or the sickness to pass. The truth is you need to use hope as your platform to help you make decisions. This means in your day-to-day life and in the most testing times, you will have an expectation for things to get better.

How can you be more hopeful? You can start by looking for more positives in a situation.

This allows you to balance the positives and negatives in life. Being grateful is also important. Be thankful for all that you have around you and make the best use of it all. Another way to boost your hope is by setting goals for yourself. The goal doesn't have to be something big. It could be as simple as writing down three things you'd like to get done that week. Start small. This will open your mind to realise you are not stuck in a crisis and that you are looking towards a brighter future of achievement and success. In regards to setting goals in life, a great quote comes to mind by the late John Osteen, who said, "I'd rather shoot high and miss it than shoot low and make it." This quote stands out to me as sometimes it's easy to be afraid to aim too high out of fear of failure. Without hope, someone like Thomas Edison would never of made the lightbulb after one thousand unsuccessful attempts. Hope opens up possibilities. Another great way to be hopeful is by spending more time in nature. Nature can add a new perspective to your problem and inspire you to think bigger than yourself.

All in all, if you want to become more hopeful, it will take effort. Although, it will improve the relationship you have with yourself. It requires you making a conscious commitment to being more hopeful in the moment of crisis. It is something you will have to work on with your inner self and act on daily. In the long term, this will bring a new sense of hope and expectation for a brighter future. This will allow you to seek and find positive change. Treat each day like an individual gift and see what doors begin to open for you.

Step Five: Be Purposeful

It's a common thing for people to say they're trying to find their purpose. They may go to great lengths to try and figure out what their purpose is in this world. To be purposeful is to continually strive towards a vision for your life. It gives you a growing confidence that you're on the right path to doing what you were created to do and a good reason to get up each morning. Being purposeful allows you to see beyond the adversities you are faced with, and it ensures you're not lead solely by your environment. Being purposeful also means in the most challenging times you can take a step back and look for meaning or lessons in the midst of the storm. You may find that your purpose lies in the talents that you've always had. Sometimes it's other people who notice your talents before you do. It could be your leadership qualities, your cooking skills, the way you fix broken things, how well you publicly speak, or many other things you look upon as normal. Your purpose is often connected to your passions.

You may think, "How can I be purposeful?" Start by asking yourself, "What is my vision for life?" By asking this, you will begin to scratch the surface on what a successful life for you looks like. This may change as years go by because you will grow, develop, and want different things. Even so, that's okay as long as you continue to have a vision for bettering yourself. Then your focus needs to turn to what's stopping you from getting to your vision. Once you figure this out, you can create a new schedule for yourself, which will include removing these distractions. By working towards your vision with a plan, you will be living purposefully.

You can use your moment of crisis as your turning point where you find your purpose in life. A crisis can shake things up in your life in such a way that you have no other choice but to reboot and re-evaluate your life. The good thing about this is in the midst of adversity, your strengths begin to develop, and your resilience builds up. The truth is if there were no tribulations in life, we wouldn't develop all the skills we have. Without all the obstacles in our way, maybe we wouldn't have found out half the things we know about ourselves. What would happen if everyone who went to the gym stopped as soon as they started to feel the slightest pain when running, squatting, or lifting weights? This would definitely hold back a lot of growth from people because as any avid gym goer knows, it's in the moments of pain where the gains are made. How can you make your crisis a growing pain? The pains and the lows you feel will be the exact thing that gives you the power to thrive in the good times.

Another way to be purposeful is to be less selfish and more giving. You can start by helping people. When you help someone without them asking, you'll get a free gift of happiness in return. There's always someone out there who could use a little help. It just depends on what you're looking for. It's like when someone falls in love with the car they just test drove, and then they suddenly keep seeing it again and again everywhere they go. Start helping others, and you will always find someone in need of help. I personally find it very gratifying when I help someone and don't expect anything in return. If everyone would do this, it would have a huge impact worldwide.

There are huge benefits to being purposeful. It has an impact on the smallest of things you do in life. Being purposeful can also be an attractive quality. It's something which allows people to see the self-respect and confidence that you have in who you are and what you were created to be. Your value of yourself shines brighter than ever when you live purposefully. You become safe and secure in your own skin. You realise that everything that tested you, or will test you in the future, just becomes part of the journey.

When you live without purpose, it's as though you lack direction to your life. It's said that lost people are harder to live with. You can tell when someone is living like a leaf in the wind and moves based on whatever is going on around them. It's important to stand for something in life. If not, it comes across as you don't see the complete value in who you are and the talents you were born with.

Let's use Lionel Messi, one of the greatest footballers of all time, as an example of being purposeful. He is the ultimate entertainer on the football pitch. When I watch him play, my jaw drops, and I say, "He is for sure a gift from God." His talent is to entertain the world with his magical footballing ability. His parents saw the talent in him from a young age, and football soon became young Messi's passion. However, he too was faced with a crisis that could have prevented him from being the player he turned out to be. At a young age, Lionel Messi was diagnosed with a hormone deficiency, which restricted his growth. This put immense pressure on his parents financially. Messi needed a growth hormone injection each night, and this came at a huge cost to his parents on a monthly basis. His parents were persistent with the treatment despite the financial difficulties. Different football teams wanted to sign Messi but couldn't afford his medical treatment. However, things changed when FC Barcelona agreed to sign Messi and pay for his medical bills as long as he moved to Spain. This was a done deal, and the 13-year-old Messi and his parents moved from Argentina to Spain, and the rest was history. Messi and his parents showed great courage when faced with adversity. Young Messi persisted through the setbacks and fulfilled what he was created to do. They don't call it the 'Magic of Messi' for no reason. Now even to this day, Messi is not one of the tallest players around. The difference is he uses his deficiency to his advantage. With his low centre of gravity, that makes it so difficult for any player to push him off of the ball. Messi is a good example that your individual gifts are made for you. Regardless of the setbacks you'll face, you need be purposeful and figure out how you can make your crisis work in your favour.

Therefore, to be purposeful in life, the journey may not always be easy. However, often the best things in life do not come so easily. One thing to realise is when you look back on life, the setbacks will be a part of what makes you who you are. So, step out in purpose and make it the centre of everything you do.

Step Six: Be Stronger

Your crisis may be your opportunity to be stronger than ever. During a crisis, it's your character that gets magnified. It's in the midst of a storm where your inner strength gets tested. It's the moments when everything on the outside seems like it's crashing down. How do you operate when the pressure is on? Pressure effects everyone differently. The high pressure moments in life put you in a prime position to transform into a stronger version of you. Pressure can affect you terribly and cause you to crumble to your knees. This is a time when people either sink or swim. You have much higher chances of being a swimmer in a crisis after following the seven steps in this book. When you overcome the obstacles you're faced with, you are taking more ownership of life and developing into your strongest self.

A crisis like a global pandemic causes a lot of people to face severe situations. It was a difficult season in life for a lot of people across the world. They faced financial strains due to jobs being lost and big companies going bankrupt. It would have caused mental health issues for many as fear was spreading rapidly across the world. Some people were scared to leave their homes without a mask and gloves to protect against the 'Invisible Enemy.' It's in a time like this where I've personally learnt important life lessons. I learnt that in a time where there was a lot of financial uncertainty, there will be some winners and some losers. With some research I found, one of the best times to invest in the stock market is after a crash. In a market crash, people start planning to make their wealth stronger by purchasing stocks with the next five to ten years in mind. When the stock market crashes, you can buy stocks at discounts up to 30 percent off or more. If your favourite clothing store was 30 percent off, you'd definitely be buying, wouldn't you? Stocks and shares are not topics I was taught growing up or had much exposure to at home, so I needed to do my own due diligence. In this crisis, I made steps to come out financially stronger. I bought shares in some companies despite all that was going on outside. A good person to gain a little more wisdom from on the stock market is Warren Buffet. If you don't know him already, he's currently one of the richest men in the world, and he has a lot of good advice for beginner investors. Buffet comes alive when there is a crisis as he knows there are a lot of opportunities to increase his net worth.

The term mental health comes to the forefront during a crisis, and, in fact, it's just as important as your financial position. I was swiftly aware of the fear and anxiousness during the global pandemic. By speaking to people, I began to recognise fear was spreading like wildfire. This was not good for my own mental health, so I decided to fight fear with faith for better times and prayed for strength for people I know during this storm. It was hard to believe what was going on. However, it is vital to believe even in the darkest of places, that more light is coming. This will allow you to ease the stress on your mind. If you can change how you think, you have the power to change your life. This can be applied to whatever goal you may have for yourself. I began to ask myself, "What's the best way to deal with a crisis?" I figured it was vital to operate with a lot of logic. Reacting purely emotionally can lead you to make a decision you may regret in years to come. But when you operate with logic, you come to an acceptance of your reality and accept that you cannot change it immediately. By accepting the reality, you can open up doors to decide what you will do from that point onwards. That way, you are taking more ownership of what you can control, which is your reaction to the problem. It's taking a more proactive than reactive approach to life. This can be a lot easier said than done for some people. However, with practice, you will find you can manage your thoughts better despite the pressure of your situation. This allows you to live with a more sound mind. To think more logically is a powerful tool to use to become stronger. This isn't encouraging you to not have or not show your emotion by any means. It simply allows you to regulate your emotions and have more balanced thoughts.

You become stronger when you are living your life with a vision. A vision is so important as it allows you to walk, talk, and live your life with more purpose. This makes you more prepared for when you are hit unexpectedly by a crisis. It's good to be prepared as this lessens the effects it can have on your life. Having a vision helps you to be stronger in the same way our bones provide strength to our body. The bone structure provides a strong framework for everything else to work around. Similar to the bone structure, a vision is what keeps you going in life and allows you to be strong when your surrounding is weak. Your vision will also face setbacks along the way, but just like a bone, it can fuse back together stronger than before. The setbacks on the way towards your vision will give you a new perspective and put you in a less comfortable position that will push you to grow. The only enemy of a vision is your own sight. Sight can hold you back and set limits on your life based on what you see in front of you. It's necessary to take that leap of faith sometimes, even when you cannot see the entire road ahead. This type of willpower to step out in uncertainty is what builds character and makes you stronger than you have ever been.

There's a very inspiring story of a woman going through a crisis, and finally taking ownership of it. She worked at a hotel as a housekeeper. She really didn't enjoy her job and felt it was making her unhappy. She attended a three-day workshop at the hotel she worked called *Reaching Your Potential*. At the end of the second day, she gifted the speaker some cookies she had baked. The woman always felt that baking was her gift in life. After tasting her cookies, the speaker felt the same and gave her some advice and a vision for a cookie business. She gave her cookies away for free to start with as the speaker recommended. Soon people started to order batches of her cookies, so she was making hundreds of cookies every week from her home kitchen. One year later, she surprised the speaker and went back to the same workshop and told her story on stage. She spoke about where she was a year ago and how she now runs a million dollar factory selling her cookies. Even the stores were beginning to stock her cookies. This wasn't something she could have imagined when she was a housekeeper at the hotel. The difference was she now had vision for her life regardless of what her current circumstances were. To start, this woman was resourceful with her time and her oven. She began selling from the back of her car. When the cookie business began to grow, she expanded to a small factory. This all started with her gaining a vision despite the crisis she was living in. When she visited the following year, she gifted the speaker with a now professionally packaged bag of her cookies and an extra gift in an envelope of ten thousand dollars. She left a note saying, "Thank you for tapping into my baking gift." I loved hearing this story. This was a great story to me as it showed you do not need to define yourself based on your current situation. The most important thing is how you plan to take ownership of it and come out stronger than ever.

So, to become stronger in difficult times, you must start with your mindset. When you adopt the mindset of, 'Every problem has a solution,' you begin to open up more possibilities for improvement. The reality is a crisis might make you have feelings of fear, depression, and frustration. Yet on the other hand, these could be the emotions that you look back in years to come as what created your life-changing moment. Your crisis could be the turning point that causes you to get out of your comfort zone and do something you've been created to do. During the tough times, it's important for you to get creative with what you have around you. You will then begin to see growth. Your new and increased level of strength will be useful in the next season of your life

Step Seven: Be Reflective

The final step for you to Own Your Crisis is to be reflective. It takes courage to be self-reflective in the best of times, much less during a crisis as it may require you to be vulnerable. Vulnerability is necessary when you are reflecting on your own actions in a situation. This means you need to make an honest judgement about yourself and decide whether you could have dealt with the situation better. When we are self-reflective, we often get the urge to not admit that we are wrong. This feeling may be telling you to practice humility in that moment. Often doing the right thing after self-reflecting is what allows you to learn from a situation and helps prevent you from making the same mistake again.

It's important to be reflective during and after a crisis to ensure you don't get consumed in the moment. One way to do this is by thinking deeply about what you've experienced. Think about the impact this is having on how you and the people around you may feel. Putting your thoughts and feelings on paper could be a progressive step for you as mentioned in step two. Another option is having a conversation with someone whose opinion you value and reflecting on their feedback. One thing I find useful is stepping outside of my own situation and taking on a third person viewpoint. This allows you to look at your difficult situation as if you aren't involved in it, and you can give yourself the honest advice you'd give a friend. Whether you decide to take the advice or not, is a whole other topic.

When you choose to be reflective, this opens doors for you to learn something about yourself in a crisis. If you look back in time, you can learn a lot from historical events. It's better to learn from the failures of others than living your life and making the same mistakes yourself. This could apply to a personal or a public crisis, like a divorce in the family or the Great Depression. From both incidents, there are lessons to be taken.

If we look at a personal crisis like a divorce in the family, this may encourage you to build a firm foundation to your relationship before you commit to marriage. Once you are in a committed relationship, you and your partner can attend a marriage preparation course. This will give you some time to address some topics you may not have discussed yet. This will also allow you to get to know your partner on a deeper level. You can find these courses online. Some are free, and some are paid courses. Seeing the effects of a divorce on the children and other family members can be quite hard. There aren't set rules on how to avoid a divorce. However, a marriage preparation course could significantly help prevent you going through the same pain.

Now if we look at a public crisis like the Great Depression, this went on from 1929 to 1939 and was widely regarded as the worse economic era ever. The rates of unemployed in America were in the multi-millions, and people's lives were severely affected due to this. People lost their jobs and were forced to rely on government relief. There are some similarities to the current global pandemic, particularly with the unemployment rates going sky high. By reflecting on an event like the Great Depression, you could aim to be better prepared financially for a crisis like this. One way you can prepare is by building more than one stream of income. Having multiple income streams gives you more financial security if one income source is lower than normal. This could provide you and your family with more financial protection and prepare you for a financial crisis.

It's great to learn from people's mistakes, but how can you be reflective in everyday life? I often take a look at what is around me. Sometimes it's right under your nose, and you don't need to look too far to find better ways of living. For example, one thing I often do is take a look at how the youngest people and the eldest people live their lives.

The youngest children (up to the age of two) are the purest and most innocent souls when they come into this world. It's only as they grow older that they are impacted by their surroundings more. When I reflect on the character of most young children, I think carefree, fearless, and joyful. Their behaviour is so clean-hearted. These are great characteristics that would release a lot of anxiousness from people's lives as they get older. In general, I think we can take a lot of advice from how pure young children are. Young children have the ability to naturally lift the mood in the most difficult situations.

At the other end of the scale of life are the elderly people. The elderly are great to be speak to as they've seen it and done it all. You can learn a lot about life by listening to and taking wisdom from someone who has had a lot of life experiences. They've been through the ups and downs in relationships, wars, financial struggles, loss of loved ones, and other life events. Yet one thing they can say is they're still standing! I personally learnt a lot from my own grandparents, who emigrated to the United Kingdom in the 1960s from the beautiful island of Jamaica. I remember asking them what it was like settling into a completely new way of life, and how they dealt with the pressures of having to provide for their children. They faced many tough moments in life, but they dealt with the tough times and always found a way for things to work. Upon reflection, I realised it's the difficult moments in life that actually build up our character and shape us into being a stronger, more resilient person. So, this is why I find it great to speak to elderly people as they've had more time to figure life out. You can cut down your learning curve by taking on some of their wisdom. This has allowed me to to focus my time and energy on the most significant things, and always choose to look at the bigger picture in life.

Ultimately, being reflective is a great way to gain more self-awareness as you'll become more aware of your own strengths and weaknesses. This is why it is crucial to be reflective during and after a crisis. By following these seven steps, you can take ownership of your crisis when it strikes. You can take valuable lessons from your crisis, find a way to come out of it stronger, and manage your mind along the way. Let's not forget that your growth happens in the storm. You have the power within you to withstand it. So, now it's time to Own Your Crisis.

Epilogue

I hope you enjoyed reading this book. During the current global pandemic, there have been restrictions on going outside as normal. So, with more time at home than before, I wrote this book to provide you with some value that will help you and never get old.

This book teaches you how to become more self-aware of how you think, and it gives you ways to take ownership of your life and the challenges it comes with. This seven-step process is transferable and applicable to many problems you may experience in life. With every problem, there is a solution. The most difficult thing is breaking your current habits and creating new ones. How can you create new habits? I encourage you to reread this book every other month for the next year. Why? Because repetition is the key to learning, and this will allow you to create new habits in your life.

My main aim with this book has been to assist you in taking ownership of your life in the toughest situations and to provide you with another reference point for when you may experience a crisis in your life. It's all about taking charge over your inner voice when it tries to keep you stuck rather than overcome the challenge and come out stronger. By taking charge of your inner voice you can live an enriched and purpose filled life.

The best thing you can do after reading this book is start living out the values you've learnt. This way, you can improve yourself but also be an example to others. Therefore, I ask you to share this message of empowerment to help someone else on their journey of life. It's important to get the message of this book out to as many people as possible. Too often people are told to keep their problems to themselves or not bring them into the workplace. With this book, you are assisted when you face a setback instead of you suffering alone.

Commit to telling at least 50 of your friends, family, and associates about this book or surprise them with a copy as a gift. This book might be exactly what they need to give their life the shift they have been waiting for. Love and blessings.

"Your Notes"

KARL DAVIS

"Your Notes"

OWN YOUR CRISIS

"Your Notes"

\---

\---

\---

\---

\---

\---

\---

\---

\---

\---

\---

\---

\---

\---

\---

\---

\---

\---

\---

\---

KARL DAVIS

"Your Notes"

OWN YOUR CRISIS

"Your Notes"

-----------------------"Your Notes"---------------

KARL DAVIS

"Your Notes"

-----------------------"Your Notes"---------------

OWN YOUR CRISIS

"Your Notes"

------------------------"Your Notes"-------------

KARL DAVIS